Mapping your Future:
Goal Setting for Personal Growth

Taylor Linton

To OK and HR, my best little buddies

Table Of Contents

Chapter 1: Introduction to Personal Development and Goals
    Understanding the Importance of Personal Development
    Setting SMART Goals
    Self-Reflection and Self-Awareness

Chapter 2: Assessing Your Skills and Interests
    Identifying Strengths and Weaknesses
    Exploring Career Options
    Aligning Goals with Passions

Chapter 3: Creating a Personal Development Plan
    Setting Short-term and Long-term Goals
    Establishing Action Steps

Chapter 4: Overcoming Obstacles and Challenges
    Dealing with Failure and Rejection
    Tracking Progress and Adjusting Goals
    Developing Resilience and Persistence
    Seeking Support and Guidance

Chapter 5: Networking and Building Relationships
    Building Professional Connections
    Networking Strategies for Young Professionals
    Mentorship and Collaboration

Chapter 6: Balancing Work and Personal Life
    Prioritizing Self-Care
    Time Management Techniques
    Setting Boundaries and Managing Stress

Chapter 7: Celebrating Success and Setting New Goals
    Reflecting on Achievements
    Setting New Challenges and Goals
    Continuing Personal Development Journey

Chapter 1: Introduction to Personal Development and Goal Setting

Understanding the Importance of Personal Development

Personal development is a crucial aspect of success in both your personal and professional life. As young adults entering the workforce, it is essential to understand the significance of personal development in achieving your goals and reaching your full potential. By focusing on self-improvement and setting personal development goals, you can enhance your skills, boost your confidence, and ultimately achieve success in your chosen career path.

One of the key reasons why personal development is important for young professionals is that it allows you to identify your strengths and weaknesses. By taking the time to assess where you excel and where you can improve, you can create a clear roadmap for personal growth. This self-awareness is vital for setting achievable goals and developing a plan to reach them. By continually working on improving yourself, you can become a more well-rounded and capable individual, which will benefit you both personally and professionally.

Furthermore, personal development helps you to build resilience and adaptability in the face of challenges and setbacks. In the fast-paced and competitive world of work, it is important to be able to bounce back from failures and setbacks. By focusing on personal development, you can develop the skills and mindset needed to overcome obstacles and keep moving forward. This resilience will not only help you navigate the ups and downs of your career but will also make you a more valuable asset to potential employers.

In addition to building resilience, personal development also plays a crucial role in enhancing your communication and interpersonal skills. As a young professional, it is essential to be able to effectively communicate with colleagues, clients, and stakeholders. By working on your personal development, you can improve your emotional intelligence, active listening, and conflict-resolution skills. These soft skills are highly valued in the workforce and can set you apart from your peers as a strong and effective communicator.

Overall, personal development is a journey of self-discovery and growth that can lead to increased happiness, fulfillment, and success in your personal and professional life. By setting personal development goals and actively working towards them, you can unlock your full potential and achieve your dreams. As you embark on your career journey, remember that personal development is not a one-time task but a lifelong process of continuous improvement. Embrace the journey, challenge yourself, and watch as you transform into the best version of yourself.

Setting SMART Goals

In order to achieve success in both your personal and professional life, it is important to set SMART goals. SMART goals are Specific, Measurable, Achievable, Relevant, and Time-bound. By setting goals that meet these criteria, you will be able to stay focused, motivated, and on track to reaching your desired outcomes.

When setting goals, it is important to be specific about what you want to achieve. This means clearly defining your goal and outlining the steps you need to take in order to reach it. For example, instead of setting a vague goal like, "I want to be successful in my career," try setting a specific goal such as, "I want to be promoted to a managerial position within the next two years."

In addition to being specific, your goals should also be measurable. This means setting concrete criteria for measuring your progress towards achieving your goal. For example, if your goal is to increase your sales performance, you could measure this by tracking the number of new clients you acquire each month.

Another important aspect of setting SMART goals is ensuring that they are achievable. While it is important to challenge yourself, setting goals that are too lofty or unrealistic can lead to feelings of frustration and failure. Make sure your goals are within reach and that you have the resources and support needed to achieve them.

It is also important to ensure that your goals are relevant to your overall personal and professional development. Ask yourself why this goal is important to you and how it aligns with your values and long-term aspirations. Setting goals that are meaningful to you will increase your motivation and commitment to achieving them.

Finally, all goals should be time-bound. This means setting a deadline for when you want to achieve your goal. Having a clear timeline will help you stay focused and motivated, as well as hold yourself accountable for taking action toward reaching your goal. By setting SMART goals, you will be able to map out your future and take the necessary steps towards personal and professional success.

Self-Reflection and Self-Awareness

Self-reflection and self-awareness are crucial components of personal development and goal setting for young professionals entering the workforce. Taking the time to reflect on your strengths, weaknesses, values, and goals can help you better understand yourself and make informed decisions about your career path. Self-awareness involves being conscious of your thoughts, feelings, and behaviors, while self-reflection involves evaluating and analyzing your experiences to learn and grow from them.

One of the first steps in developing self-awareness is to engage in self-reflection activities, such as journaling, meditation, or talking to a mentor or coach. These activities can help you gain insights into your values, beliefs, and motivations, which can guide your career decisions and goal-setting. By understanding your strengths and weaknesses, you can leverage your skills and work on areas for improvement to achieve your career goals.

Self-awareness also involves being mindful of your emotions and reactions in different situations. By practicing self-awareness, you can better manage stress, communicate effectively with others, and build meaningful relationships in the workplace. Being self-aware can also help you take ownership of your actions and behavior, leading to increased accountability and personal growth.

In addition to self-reflection and self-awareness, setting specific, measurable, achievable, relevant, and time-bound (SMART) goals is essential for young professionals entering the workforce. By setting clear goals for your career development, you can stay motivated, focused, and on track to achieve success. Regularly reviewing and adjusting your goals based on your self-reflection and self-awareness can help you stay aligned with your values and priorities.

In conclusion, self-reflection and self-awareness are valuable tools for personal development and goal setting for young professionals entering the workforce. By taking the time to understand yourself, your values, and your goals, you can make informed decisions about your career path and take steps toward achieving success. Cultivating self-awareness and setting SMART goals can help you navigate the challenges of the workplace, build meaningful relationships, and create a fulfilling and rewarding career.

Chapter 2: Assessing Your Skills and Interests

Identifying Strengths and Weaknesses

In order to successfully navigate the challenges of the workforce, it is crucial for young adults to identify their strengths and weaknesses. Understanding what you excel at and where you may need improvement can help you set realistic goals and develop a plan for personal growth. This subchapter will guide you through the process of self-assessment and provide tools to help you identify your unique strengths and weaknesses.

One of the first steps in identifying your strengths and weaknesses is to reflect on your past experiences. Take note of situations where you felt confident and performed well, as these are likely areas of strength for you. On the other hand, think about times when you struggled or received feedback for improvement, as these can indicate areas where you may need to focus on personal development. By analyzing past experiences, you can gain valuable insights into your abilities and areas for growth.

Another important aspect of identifying strengths and weaknesses is seeking feedback from others. Ask friends, family members, teachers, or colleagues for their perspective on your strengths and areas for improvement. Their input can provide a different perspective and help you identify blind spots that you may not have been aware of. Additionally, consider taking assessments or personality tests to gain a better understanding of your strengths and weaknesses from a more objective standpoint.

Once you have identified your strengths and weaknesses, it is important to create a plan for personal development. Set specific, measurable goals that align with your strengths and address your areas for improvement. For example, if you excel at communication but struggle with time management, you may set a goal to improve your time management skills by implementing time-blocking techniques or using a productivity app. By setting clear goals and actionable steps, you can work towards continuous improvement and personal growth.

In conclusion, identifying your strengths and weaknesses is a critical step in personal development and goal setting for young professionals entering the workforce. By reflecting on past experiences, seeking feedback from others, and creating a plan for development, you can leverage your strengths to achieve success and address areas for improvement. Remember that personal growth is a lifelong journey, and by consistently assessing and developing your skills, you can continue to progress and achieve your goals in the workplace and beyond.

Exploring Career Options

As young adults entering the workforce, one of the most important tasks you will face is exploring your career options. It can be overwhelming to think about the multitude of paths available to you, but taking the time to explore your options is crucial in finding a career that aligns with your interests, skills, and values. In this subchapter, we will discuss the importance of exploring career options and provide you with some strategies to help you navigate this process.

One of the first steps in exploring career options is to assess your interests and skills. What are you passionate about? What activities do you enjoy doing in your free time? What are your strengths and weaknesses? By taking the time to reflect on these questions, you can start to identify potential career paths that align with your interests and abilities. Consider taking career assessment tests or speaking with a career counselor to gain further insights into potential career options.

Networking is another key component of exploring career options. Building relationships with professionals in industries that interest you can provide valuable insights and opportunities. Attend industry events, join professional organizations, and reach out to individuals working in fields that you are curious about. Informational interviews can be a great way to learn more about different career paths and gain valuable advice from industry professionals.

It's important to keep an open mind when exploring career options. You may discover new career paths that you had never considered before, or you may find that your interests and priorities change as you gain more experience in the workforce. Don't be afraid to try out different roles or industries to see what resonates with you. Remember, your career is a journey, and it's okay to explore different paths before settling on a long-term career goal.

Finally, setting goals and creating a plan for your career exploration can help you stay focused and motivated. Identify short-term and long-term goals for your career development, and create a timeline for achieving them. Keep track of your progress and make adjustments to your plan as needed. By actively exploring your career options and setting goals for your personal development, you can pave the way for a fulfilling and successful career in the future.

Aligning Goals with Passions

In order to achieve success in your career, it is essential to align your goals with your passions. When your goals are in line with what truly excites and motivates you, you are more likely to stay committed and dedicated to achieving them. Young adults entering the workforce need to take the time to identify their passions and determine how they can incorporate them into their career goals.

One way to align your goals with your passions is to take a step back and reflect on what truly makes you happy and fulfilled. Think about the activities that you enjoy doing in your free time and consider how you can incorporate those interests into your professional life. By aligning your career goals with your passions, you will be more likely to find fulfillment and satisfaction in your work.

Another way to align your goals with your passions is to set specific and achievable goals that are in line with what you are passionate about. By setting clear objectives that align with your passions, you will be more motivated to work towards achieving them. This will also help you stay focused and determined in the face of challenges or setbacks.

It is also important to seek out mentors and role models who have successfully aligned their goals with their passions. By learning from others who have achieved success in pursuing their passions, you can gain valuable insights and guidance on how to do the same. Surrounding yourself with like-minded individuals who share similar passions can also provide support and encouragement as you work towards achieving your goals.

In conclusion, aligning your goals with your passions is essential for personal development and success in your career. By taking the time to identify your passions and set goals that align with them, you can increase your motivation and commitment to achieving success. Seek out mentors and role models who have successfully aligned their goals with their passions and surround yourself with like-minded individuals who can provide support and encouragement along the way. By aligning your goals with your passions, you can create a fulfilling and successful career that brings you joy and satisfaction.

Chapter 3: Creating a Personal Development Plan

Setting Short-term and Long-term Goals

Setting short-term and long-term goals is an essential step in achieving success in both your personal and professional life. As young adults entering the workforce, it is crucial to have a clear vision of where you want to go and how you plan to get there. By setting specific, measurable, achievable, relevant, and time-bound goals, you can create a roadmap for your future success.

Short-term goals are those that you can accomplish within a relatively short period, typically within a few weeks or months. These goals are important as they help you stay focused and motivated in the short term. Examples of short-term goals may include completing a training course, networking with industry professionals, or gaining a new skill relevant to your field. By setting short-term goals, you can track your progress and make adjustments as needed to stay on track toward your long-term objectives.

Long-term goals, on the other hand, are those that you aspire to achieve over a more extended period, typically within one to five years or even longer. These goals provide direction and purpose to your actions, helping you stay committed to your vision of success. Examples of long-term goals may include obtaining a promotion, starting your own business, or achieving financial independence. By setting long-term goals, you can create a clear path towards your ultimate aspirations and work towards fulfilling your full potential.

When setting goals, it is essential to ensure that they are SMART – specific, measurable, achievable, relevant, and time-bound. Specific goals are clear and well-defined, making it easier to create a plan of action. Measurable goals allow you to track your progress and celebrate your achievements along the way. Achievable goals are realistic and within your reach, keeping you motivated and engaged in the process. Relevant goals are meaningful and aligned with your values and aspirations, giving you a sense of purpose and direction. Time-bound goals have a deadline for completion, helping you stay focused and accountable for your progress.

Setting short-term and long-term goals is a critical component of personal development and goal setting for young professionals entering the workforce. By creating a roadmap for your future success, you can stay focused, motivated, and committed to achieving your aspirations.

Whether you are setting short-term goals to track your progress or long-term goals to fulfill your ultimate vision of success, remember to make your goals SMART to ensure they are specific, measurable, achievable, relevant, and time-bound. With a clear vision and a plan of action, you can map out your future and reach your full potential as a young professional.

Establishing Action Steps

As young adults entering the workforce, it is important to establish clear action steps towards achieving your personal development goals. By mapping out the steps you need to take, you can create a roadmap for success and stay focused on your objectives.

The first step in establishing action steps is to clearly define your goals. Take the time to reflect on what you want to achieve in your personal and professional life. Whether it's advancing in your career, improving your communication skills, or fostering better relationships, be specific about what you want to accomplish.

Once you have identified your goals, break them down into smaller, more manageable tasks. This will help you stay organized and make progress towards your objectives. Create a timeline for each task and set deadlines to hold yourself accountable. By breaking your goals into smaller steps, you can track your progress and adjust your actions as needed.

By being flexible and willing to adjust your goals as needed, you can adapt to changing circumstances and stay on track towards achieving your long- term objectives. Remember, goals are meant to be dynamic and should be revised as necessary to reflect your growth and development as a young professional.

Chapter 4: Overcoming Obstacles and Challenges

Dealing with Failure and Rejection

Dealing with failure and rejection is an inevitable part of life, especially for young adults who are just starting their careers. It's important to remember that setbacks are not the end of the road, but rather opportunities for growth and learning. When faced with failure or rejection, it's crucial to maintain a positive mindset and not let it discourage you from pursuing your goals.

One way to cope with failure and rejection is to reframe your mindset. Instead of viewing setbacks as personal shortcomings, see them as opportunities to learn and improve. Reflect on what went wrong and what you can do differently in the future. By approaching failure with a growth mindset, you can turn setbacks into steppingstones towards success.

Another important aspect of dealing with failure and rejection is to seek support from others. Talk to friends, family, or mentors about your experiences and how you're feeling. Surround yourself with people who believe in you and can offer encouragement and advice.

Remember that you're not alone in facing setbacks, and there are people who are willing to help you through tough times.

It's also essential to practice self-care when dealing with failure and rejection. Take time to prioritize your mental and emotional well-being by engaging in activities that bring you joy and relaxation. Whether it's exercise, meditation, or spending time with loved ones, self-care can help you recharge and bounce back from setbacks with renewed energy and perspective.

Next, prioritize your action steps based on their importance and impact on your overall goals. Focus on completing high-priority tasks first to make the most significant progress toward your objectives. Remember to be flexible and adjust your priorities as needed to stay on track.

Lastly, it is important to regularly review and reassess your action steps to ensure you are making progress towards your goals. Reflect on what is working well and what could be improved, and make adjustments as needed. By staying focused and committed to your action steps, you can achieve your personal development goals and set yourself up for success in your career and beyond.

Tracking Progress and Adjusting Goals

Tracking progress and adjusting goals are essential components of personal development and goal setting for young professionals entering the workforce. In this subchapter, we will explore the importance of monitoring your progress towards your goals and making adjustments as needed to ensure success.

One of the key reasons for tracking progress is to hold yourself accountable for the goals you have set. By regularly reviewing your progress, you can identify any areas where you may be falling short and take corrective action. This helps you stay focused and motivated as you work towards achieving your goals.

Additionally, tracking progress allows you to celebrate your successes along the way. Recognizing the milestones you have reached can boost your confidence and reinforce your commitment to your goals. It also provides an opportunity to reflect on what has worked well and what can be improved upon in the future.

Adjusting goals is another crucial aspect of personal development and goal setting. As you gain new experiences and insights in the workforce, your priorities and aspirations may evolve. It is important to regularly reassess your goals to ensure they align with your current values and aspirations.

Lastly, remember that failure and rejection are not the end of the road, but rather detours on the path to success. Keep your goals in mind and stay focused on your personal development journey. By learning from setbacks, seeking support, practicing self-care, and maintaining a positive mindset, you can navigate through failure and rejection with resilience and determination.

Developing Resilience and Persistence

In today's fast-paced and competitive world, developing resilience and persistence is crucial for young adults who are just entering the workforce. The ability to bounce back from setbacks and stay committed to your goals is what will set you apart from your peers and help you achieve success in your career. In this subchapter, we will explore some key strategies for developing resilience and persistence that will help you navigate the challenges and obstacles that you may face in your professional journey.

One of the first steps in developing resilience and persistence is to cultivate a growth mindset. This means viewing challenges as opportunities for growth and learning, rather than as insurmountable obstacles. By adopting a positive attitude and believing in your ability to overcome difficulties, you will be better equipped to persevere in the face of adversity and achieve your goals.

Another important aspect of developing resilience and persistence is setting realistic and achievable goals. By breaking down your long-term objectives into smaller, manageable steps, you can track your progress and stay motivated along the way. Remember that setbacks are a natural part of any journey, and it's important to stay focused on your ultimate goal, even when things don't go as planned.

In addition to setting goals, it's also important to build a support network of mentors, colleagues, and friends who can provide guidance and encouragement when you need it most. Surrounding yourself with positive influences and seeking help when necessary can help you stay motivated and maintain your resilience in the face of challenges.

Finally, remember to practice self-care and prioritize your well-being as you work towards your goals. Taking care of your physical and mental health will help you stay resilient and persistent in the face of stress and pressure. By incorporating these strategies into your daily routine, you can develop the resilience and persistence needed to succeed in your career and achieve your personal development goals.

Seeking Support and Guidance

As young adults entering the workforce, it is important to seek support and guidance as you navigate this new chapter in your life. Seeking support from mentors, colleagues, and even friends and family can provide invaluable insight and advice as you work towards your personal development goals.

These individuals can offer different perspectives and help you see things from a new angle, which can be instrumental in setting and achieving your goals.

One of the best ways to seek support and guidance is by finding a mentor in your field of interest. A mentor can provide you with valuable insights, advice, and guidance based on their own experiences and expertise. They can help you set realistic goals, create a roadmap for achieving them, and hold you accountable along the way. By building a strong relationship with a mentor, you can accelerate your personal development and reach your goals faster than you ever thought possible.

In addition to seeking support from a mentor, it is also important to surround yourself with a supportive network of colleagues, friends, and family members. These individuals can offer encouragement, motivation, and a listening ear when you need it most. By building a strong support system, you can stay focused on your goals and overcome any challenges that may come your way.

When seeking support and guidance, it is important to be open and receptive to feedback and advice. While it can be difficult to hear criticism or suggestions for improvement, it is important to remember that these comments are meant to help you grow and develop. By being open to feedback, you can learn from your mistakes, make adjustments to your goals, and continue to progress towards your personal development objectives.

In conclusion, seeking support and guidance is a crucial aspect of personal development and goal setting for young professionals entering the workforce. By finding a mentor, building a strong support network, and being open to feedback and advice, you can accelerate your growth and achieve your goals more effectively. Remember, you don't have to navigate this journey alone – there are people around you who are eager to help you succeed.

Chapter 5: Networking and Building Relationships

Building Professional Connections

Building professional connections is a crucial aspect of personal development and goal setting for young professionals entering the workforce. These connections can open doors to new opportunities, provide mentorship, and help you navigate the complexities of your chosen career path. In this subchapter, we will explore the importance of building professional connections and provide tips on how to do so effectively.

One of the key benefits of building professional connections is the potential for career advancement. By networking with individuals in your industry, you can learn about job openings, gain insights into different companies, and even secure referrals. These connections can also serve as mentors, offering valuable advice and guidance as you navigate your career. By surrounding yourself with successful and experienced professionals, you can learn from their experiences and avoid common pitfalls.

In addition to career advancement, building professional connections can also help you stay current in your field. By attending industry events, joining professional organizations, and connecting with colleagues on social media, you can stay informed about the latest trends and developments in your industry. This can give you a competitive edge and help you position yourself as a thought leader in your field.

When it comes to building professional connections, quality is often more important than quantity. Instead of trying to connect with as many people as possible, focus on building meaningful relationships with individuals who share your values and goals. Take the time to get to know them on a personal level and show genuine interest in their work and accomplishments. By building strong, authentic connections, you can create a network of trusted allies who will support you throughout your career.

In conclusion, building professional connections is a vital aspect of personal development and goal setting for young professionals. By networking with individuals in your industry, you can open doors to new opportunities, gain valuable insights, and stay current in your field. Focus on building quality relationships with individuals who share your values and goals, and invest time and effort into nurturing these connections. By doing so, you can create a strong network of allies who will support you as you navigate your career path.

Networking Strategies for Young Professionals

Networking is a crucial aspect of personal development and goal setting for young professionals entering the workforce. It involves building relationships with people in your industry or field of interest in order to create opportunities for growth and advancement in your career. In this subchapter, we will explore some effective networking strategies that young professionals can use to establish meaningful connections and achieve their professional goals.

One key networking strategy for young professionals is to attend industry events and conferences. These events provide a valuable opportunity to meet and connect with people who work in your desired field. By attending workshops, panels, and networking sessions, you can gain insights into the industry, learn about current trends and challenges, and make valuable contacts that can help you advance your career.

Another effective networking strategy is to leverage social media platforms such as LinkedIn to connect with professionals in your industry. By creating a strong online presence and actively engaging with others in your field, you can expand your network, stay up to date on industry news, and showcase your skills and expertise to potential employers or collaborators. Remember to keep your profile professional and up-to-date, and engage with others by commenting on their posts, sharing relevant content, and reaching out to connect.

Networking within your own organization is also important for young professionals. Building relationships with colleagues, supervisors, and mentors can help you gain valuable insights into company culture, industry trends, and career advancement opportunities. By seeking out opportunities to collaborate on projects, offer assistance, and participate in company events, you can demonstrate your value as a team player and build a strong network of support within your organization.

In addition to traditional networking strategies, young professionals can also benefit from seeking out mentorship opportunities. Finding a mentor who has experience and expertise in your desired field can provide valuable guidance, support, and insights into career development. By establishing a mentor-mentee relationship, you can gain valuable advice, feedback, and connections that can help you navigate challenges, set goals, and achieve success in your career.

Overall, networking is a critical component of personal development and goal setting for young professionals. By actively engaging with others in your industry, attending events, leveraging social media, and seeking out mentorship opportunities, you can build a strong network of support, gain valuable insights, and create opportunities for growth and advancement in your career. Remember to approach networking with authenticity, curiosity, and a willingness to learn from others, and you will be well on your way to achieving your professional goals.

Mentorship and Collaboration

Mentorship and collaboration are two key components of success in any career, especially for young adults who are just starting out in the workforce. Finding a mentor who can provide guidance, support, and advice can make a significant impact on your professional development. A mentor can help you navigate the challenges of the workplace, provide valuable insights into your chosen field, and help you set and achieve your career goals.

Collaborating with colleagues, on the other hand, can help you build strong professional relationships, expand your network, and work more effectively as part of a team.

When it comes to mentorship, it's important to seek out someone who you admire and respect in your field. This person should be willing to share their knowledge and experience with you, provide constructive feedback, and help you grow as a professional. Remember that mentorship is a two-way street - be sure to show appreciation for your mentor's time and expertise and be open to learning from their insights and advice.

Collaboration, on the other hand, is all about working together with your colleagues to achieve common goals. By collaborating with others, you can leverage each other's strengths, share ideas and resources, and support each other in reaching your objectives. Effective collaboration requires communication, trust, and a willingness to compromise. By working together with your colleagues, you can accomplish more than you ever could on your own.

In today's fast-paced and competitive job market, mentorship and collaboration are more important than ever for young professionals. By seeking out mentors who can provide guidance and support, and by collaborating with colleagues to achieve common goals, you can enhance your personal development and set yourself up for success in your career. Remember to always be open to learning from others, to communicate effectively with your peers, and to work together towards shared objectives. With mentorship and collaboration, the possibilities for growth and success are endless.

Chapter 6: Balancing Work and Personal Life

Prioritizing Self-Care

Prioritizing self-care is essential for young adults who are entering the workforce and navigating the challenges of personal development and goal setting. In today's fast-paced world, it can be easy to neglect our own well- being in favor of achieving professional success. However, taking care of ourselves is crucial for maintaining a healthy work-life balance and ensuring long-term success in our careers.

One of the first steps in prioritizing self-care is recognizing the importance of setting boundaries. This means learning to say no to tasks or commitments that do not align with your personal goals and values. By setting boundaries, you can protect your time and energy, allowing you to focus on activities that truly matter to you. This could mean setting aside time each day for exercise, meditation, or other activities that help you recharge and stay centered.

Another key aspect of self-care is practicing mindfulness. Mindfulness involves being fully present in the moment and paying attention to your thoughts, feelings, and sensations without judgment. By practicing mindfulness, you can reduce stress, improve your focus, and enhance your overall well-being. This could involve taking a few minutes each day to practice deep breathing exercises or incorporating mindfulness techniques into your daily routine.

In addition to setting boundaries and practicing mindfulness, it is important to prioritize physical health as part of your self-care routine. This could involve eating a balanced diet, getting regular exercise, and getting an adequate amount of sleep each night. Taking care of your physical health can have a profound impact on your mental and emotional well-being, helping you to feel more energized and focused throughout the workday.

Self-care also involves taking the time to nurture your relationships and social connections. Building strong relationships with friends, family, and colleagues can provide you with a support system to lean on during challenging times. This could involve scheduling regular social activities, reaching out to loved ones for support, or participating in networking events to expand your professional circle. By prioritizing self-care and nurturing your relationships, you can build a strong foundation for personal development and goal-setting as you navigate the challenges of entering the workforce as a young adult.

Time Management Techniques

In today's fast-paced world, time management is a crucial skill for young professionals entering the workforce. Without effective time management techniques, it can be easy to feel overwhelmed and fall behind on important tasks. In this subchapter, we will explore some key strategies that can help you make the most of your time and achieve your personal development goals.

One of the most important time management techniques is prioritizing your tasks. Before you start your day, take a few minutes to create a to-do list and rank your tasks in order of importance. This will help you focus on the most critical tasks first and ensure that you are making progress towards your goals. By prioritizing your tasks, you can avoid getting bogged down in less important activities and stay on track for success.

Another effective time management technique is to break large tasks into smaller, more manageable chunks. When faced with a daunting project, it can be easy to procrastinate and put off getting started. By breaking the task into smaller pieces, you can make progress more easily and build momentum towards completing the project. This approach can help you stay motivated and on track, even when faced with challenging tasks.

Setting deadlines for yourself is another key time management technique that can help you stay on track and achieve your goals. By setting specific deadlines for each task on your to-do list, you can create a sense of urgency and accountability that will help you stay focused and motivated. Deadlines can also help you prioritize your tasks and ensure that you are making progress towards your personal development goals.

Finally, it's important to remember that time management is not just about getting things done quickly, but also about taking care of yourself. Make sure to schedule time for breaks, exercise, and relaxation to avoid burnout and maintain your wellbeing. By taking care of yourself and managing your time effectively, you can achieve your personal development goals and thrive in your career as a young professional.

Setting Boundaries and Managing Stress

Setting boundaries and managing stress are essential skills for young adults entering the workforce. As you navigate the demands of a new job, it's important to establish clear boundaries to protect your time and energy.

This means learning to say no when necessary, setting limits on how much work you take on, and prioritizing self-care. By setting boundaries, you can avoid burnout and maintain a healthy work-life balance.

One effective way to set boundaries is to communicate openly and honestly with your colleagues and superiors. Let them know your limits and expectations and be assertive in advocating for yourself. Remember that it's okay to say no to additional projects or tasks if you feel overwhelmed. By setting boundaries early on, you can establish a healthy work environment that respects your needs and allows you to perform at your best.

Managing stress is another crucial aspect of personal development for young professionals. The demands of a new job can be overwhelming, but learning to cope with stress in a healthy way is essential for long-term success. Take time to identify your stress triggers and develop strategies for managing them, such as practicing mindfulness, exercising, or seeking support from friends and family.

In addition to setting boundaries and managing stress, it's important to set clear goals for your personal and professional development. By defining your long-term objectives and breaking them down into manageable steps, you can create a roadmap for success. Set SMART goals that are specific, measurable, achievable, relevant, and time-bound, and track your progress regularly to stay motivated and focused.

In conclusion, setting boundaries, managing stress, and goal setting are key components of personal development for young professionals entering the workforce. By mastering these skills, you can build a strong foundation for success in your career and personal life. Remember to prioritize self-care, communicate assertively, and stay focused on your goals to achieve your full potential.

Chapter 7: Celebrating Success and Setting New Goals

Reflecting on Achievements

Reflecting on Achievements is an important aspect of personal development and goal setting for young professionals entering the workforce. Taking the time to look back on your accomplishments can provide valuable insights into your strengths, areas for improvement, and overall progress toward your career goals. By reflecting on your achievements, you can gain a better understanding of where you excel and where you may need to focus more attention in order to continue growing and advancing in your career.

One way to reflect on your achievements is to keep a journal or list of your accomplishments. This can include both big wins, such as landing a new job or receiving a promotion, as well as smaller victories, like completing a challenging project or receiving positive feedback from a colleague. By documenting your achievements, you can track your progress over time and see how far you've come since you first started working towards your goals.

Another way to reflect on your achievements is to seek feedback from others, such as mentors, colleagues, or supervisors. Asking for feedback can provide you with valuable insights into how others perceive your work and can help you identify areas where you may need to improve. By being open to feedback and willing to learn from others, you can continue to grow and develop as a professional.

Reflecting on your achievements can also help you set new goals and create a roadmap for your future success. By looking back on what you have already accomplished, you can gain a better understanding of what you are capable of and where you want to go next in your career. Setting new goals based on your past achievements can help you stay motivated and focused as you continue to work towards your long-term objectives.

In conclusion, reflecting on your achievements is an essential part of personal development and goal setting for young professionals entering the workforce. By taking the time to look back on your accomplishments, you can gain valuable insights into your strengths, areas for improvement, and overall progress toward your career goals. By keeping a journal, seeking feedback from others, and setting new goals based on your past achievements, you can continue to grow and develop as a professional and work towards achieving your dreams.

Setting New Challenges and Goals

As young adults enter the workforce, it is important to continually set new challenges and goals for yourself in order to continue growing and developing both personally and professionally. Setting new challenges can help you push yourself outside of your comfort zone, learn new skills, and ultimately achieve success in your chosen career path. In this subchapter, we will explore the importance of setting new challenges and goals, as well as provide tips on how to effectively set and achieve them.

One of the key benefits of setting new challenges and goals is that it gives you a sense of direction and purpose in your career. By identifying what you want to achieve and setting specific goals to work towards, you can stay focused and motivated to take the necessary steps to reach your desired outcome. This sense of purpose can help you overcome obstacles and setbacks along the way, as you have a clear vision of where you are headed and what you need to do to get there.

Another benefit of setting new challenges and goals is that it can help you expand your skill set and knowledge base. By pushing yourself to try new things and take on tasks that may be outside of your comfort zone, you can develop new skills and learn valuable lessons that will benefit you in your career. Whether it's learning a new programming language, taking on a leadership role in a project, or volunteering for a challenging assignment, setting new challenges can help you grow and develop as a young professional.

In order to effectively set and achieve new challenges and goals, it is important to make them specific, measurable, achievable, relevant, and time-bound (SMART). By setting SMART goals, you can clearly define what you want to achieve, how you will measure your progress, and when you aim to accomplish it. This can help you stay accountable and track your progress as you work towards achieving your goals.

Setting new challenges and goals is essential for personal development and growth as a young professional entering the workforce. By identifying what you want to achieve, pushing yourself outside of your comfort zone, and setting SMART goals, you can stay focused, motivated, and on track to achieving success in your career. Remember that challenges and setbacks are a natural part of the journey, but by setting new goals and staying committed to your development, you can continue to grow and thrive in your chosen field.

Continuing Personal Development Journey

As young adults embark on their journey into the workforce, it is important to recognize that personal development is an ongoing process that never truly ends. In fact, it is crucial to continue setting goals and working towards self-improvement in order to achieve success and fulfillment in both your personal and professional life. This subchapter will explore the concept of continuing personal development and provide practical tips for young professionals to continue their growth and development.

One key aspect of continuing personal development is the willingness to step outside of your comfort zone. This means taking on new challenges, learning new skills, and pushing yourself to grow in ways that may be uncomfortable at first. By continuously challenging yourself, you will not only expand your knowledge and abilities, but you will also build resilience and adaptability, which are essential traits for success in the fast-paced world of work.

Another important component of continuing personal development is the practice of reflection. Take the time to reflect on your experiences, successes, and failures in order to learn from them and make adjustments moving forward. This can involve journaling, engaging in self-assessment exercises, or seeking feedback from mentors or peers. By reflecting on your journey, you can gain valuable insights into your strengths and weaknesses, allowing you to make informed decisions about your personal and professional development goals.

Setting specific, measurable, achievable, relevant, and time-bound (SMART) goals is another essential aspect of continuing personal development. By setting clear goals and creating a plan for achieving them, you can stay focused and motivated as you work towards your objectives. It is important to regularly review and adjust your goals as needed, in order to ensure that they remain relevant and aligned with your long-term aspirations.

Finally, seeking out opportunities for growth and development is vital for young professionals who are committed to continuing their personal development journey. This can involve taking on new projects, pursuing further education or training, attending workshops or conferences, or seeking out mentorship and coaching. By actively seeking out opportunities for growth, you can expand your knowledge, skills, and network, positioning yourself for success in your career and personal life. Remember, personal development is a lifelong journey, and by staying committed to your growth and development, you can unlock your full potential and achieve your goals.

Afterword

    Thank you so much for taking the time to read my book. I have had many struggles with my own personal growth and have seen the uncertainty with all those younger than me working to find a life that they find passion living. My goal with this book was to provide my little bit of knowledge to those younger than I in the hopes that it helps just one of them on their path to living a more fulfilling life. If you found this book helpful or motivating please leave a review or reach out to me directly through social media. I'd love to hear your experience with it. Thanks!

- Taylor L

www.ingramcontent.com/pod-product-compliance
Lightning Source LLC
Chambersburg PA
CBHW030055230526
45471CB00003B/1111